Oxford Read and Discover

Helping
Around the World

Sarah Medina

Contents

OXFORD
UNIVERSITY PRESS

OXFORD

UNIVERSITY PRESS

Great Clarendon Street, Oxford OX2 6DP

Oxford University Press is a department of the University of Oxford. It furthers the University's objective of excellence in research, scholarship, and education by publishing worldwide in

Oxford New York

Auckland Cape Town Dar es Salaam Hong Kong Karachi Kuala Lumpur Madrid Melbourne Mexico City Nairobi New Delhi Shanghai Taipei Toronto

With offices in

Argentina Austria Brazil Chile Czech Republic France Greece Guatemala Hungary Italy Japan Poland Portugal Singapore South Korea Switzerland Thailand Turkey Ukraine Vietnam

OXFORD and OXFORD ENGLISH are registered trade marks of Oxford University Press in the UK and in certain other countries

© Oxford University Press 2010

The moral rights of the author have been asserted

Database right Oxford University Press (maker)

First published 2010

2019

15

ISBN: 978 0 19 464562 1

An Audio Pack containing this book and an Audio download is also available, ISBN 978 0 19 402247 7

This book is also available as an e-Book, ISBN 978 0 19 464734 2

An accompanying Activity Book is also available, ISBN 978 0 19 464572 0

Printed in China

This book is printed on paper from certified and well-managed sources.

ACKNOWLEDGEMENTS

Illustrations by: Kelly Kennedy pp.5, 15, 29; Dusan Pavlic/ Beehive Illustration pp.38, 46; Gary Swift p.46 (whale)

The Publishers would also like to thank the following for their kind permission to reproduce photographs and other copyright material: Alamy pp.3 and 9 (INTERFOTO/teacher), 10 (Trappe/Caro), 11 (Gary Cook), 17 (Mike Goldwater), 25 (Thomas Semmler), 29 (Jeff Greenberg/Peter Arnold, Inc), 30 (Joe Sohm/Visions of America, LLC), 31 (Ulrich Niehoff/imagebroker/insect hotel); Corbis pp.3 (Howard Davies/doctor), 4 (Jeremy Horner), 7 (Howard Davies), 15 (Kim Ludbrook/epa), 18 (Anna Clopet), 19 (Amit Dave/Reuters), 21 (Charles Caratini/Sygma); Getty Images pp.3 (Greg Wood/AFP/leopard, Kim Jae-Hwan/AFP/ beach), 5 (Hans Neleman/Stone), 22 (Paula Bronstein/Getty Images News), 23 (Juan Barreto/AFP), 24 (Greg Wood/AFP), 26 (Bradley Kanaris/bird cleaning), 27 (Tony Ashby/AFP), 33 (Kim Jae-Hwan/AFP); Nature Picture Library pp.26 (Lukasseck/ ARCO/orang-utans); Oxford University Press pp.6, 8, 13, 16, 32; Photolibrary pp.31 (Peter Bennett/Ambient Images/planting), 34 (RESO RESO), 35 (Tsuneo Nakamura); Press Association Images p.14 (Tomas Stargardter/AP); Reuters Pictures p.20 (Adrees Latif); Still Pictures pp.12 (Shehzad Noorani/ Majority World), 28 (Bruno Loisel/BIOSphoto); Vestergaard Frandsen p.18 (LifeStraw in use in Northern Uganda).

Introduction

All around the world, people help each other. Many people, like doctors and teachers, have jobs that help others. They are paid money for their work. Lots of people give their time freely to do work to help others. They are called volunteers.

What are these people doing?
Do you know people who do work to help others?
Are there volunteers where you live? What do they do?
Would you like a job that helps others?

Now read and discover more about helping around the world!

Caring for Others

Surgeons at Work, Japan

It's wonderful to care for a sick child who needs help. It's amazing to save someone's life! Many people do jobs that care for others.

Doctors and Nurses

Workers like doctors and nurses are very important. They help people to stay healthy, and they care for people who are sick.

Doctors often work in clinics or hospitals, and they find out why people are sick, and help them to get better. Some doctors called surgeons do difficult operations. Nurses work with doctors. They give medication, and care for sick people and their families. In some schools, there's a nurse to help children who are sick or who have an accident.

Helping People Through Life

The people who bring babies into the world are called midwives. They also help the baby, mother, and father to be well, in hospital or at home.

Children and adults get help from doctors and nurses in schools, clinics, and hospitals. They can have vaccinations and they can learn about being healthy. They can also go to the dentist to care for their teeth and mouth.

Discover!

Every year, about 130 million babies are born around the world. That's about 250 babies every minute of every day!

It's important to stay healthy. We should care for our body from when we are young to when we are old. If we eat well, and walk or do sport, we probably won't get sick very often. We can help ourselves to stay healthy. Others can help us, too, if we are sick or disabled, or if we have an accident.

When people are old, sick, or disabled, they often need help with cooking, cleaning, shopping, washing clothes, and taking medication. They can get help at home from other people in the family, or from care workers. Sometimes they have to live in a care home.

When people are going to die, they sometimes stay in a hospice. Hospice workers can help people a lot at the end of their life.

Caring for a Parent at Home

Voluntary Work

A Volunteer Doctor, Macedonia

In many countries, the government helps to care for people. Governments give money to workers like doctors and nurses. Sometimes, when there isn't enough money, more help is needed. More help is needed after an emergency, too. Volunteers give this help. Anyone can do voluntary work. Volunteers can be young or old! Many volunteers work with charities that help people all around the world.

Some doctors and nurses fly thousands of kilometers to do voluntary work in another country. They work in hospitals or clinics for many weeks or months. They sometimes give vaccinations so that people do not get serious diseases.

Discover!

Every year in the USA, about 62 million people do voluntary work. About 8 million volunteers are 16 to 24 years old.

→ Go to pages 36–37 for activities.

7

2 Teaching Others

People who teach others do one of the most important jobs. Education helps people to get a better job and to have a better life. Education is important for everyone.

At Home

When we are very young, we don't know much about anything! Our parents and other people in our family teach us many things at home. Before we go to school, they help us to eat, walk, talk, and play. They help us as much as possible at the start of our life.

Teaching Children at School, Nepal

At School

School teachers have a very special, important job. They get children ready for adult life. School teachers help very young children to read and write, and to do art and simple mathematics. They also teach older children subjects like geography, history, science, and languages.

Many other people help in schools. Classroom assistants give more help to children who need it, for example, children who are disabled. In some schools, cooks make snacks and lunch for children and their teachers. Playground assistants help children to stay safe when they are in the playground.

Sadly, many people in the world can't have a good education. Today, only about 82% of people who are more than 15 years old can read and write.

At College and University

Education isn't just for children. After school, many young people go to college or university. Some people go to college or university when they are older adults. Others study different subjects at home after work.

Professors teach college and university students many different subjects – from architecture to zoology! One of the most popular university subjects is law. Professors need to know a lot about their subject so that they can help students to do well and get better jobs through life.

Discover!

One of the biggest universities is Indira Gandhi National Open University in India. It has about two million students!

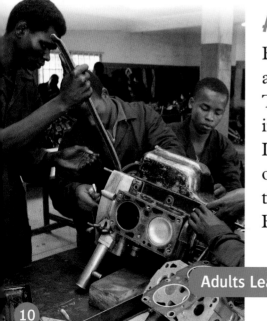

At Work

Education doesn't stop after college or university. Trainers teach workers new information, for example, Information Technology or a new language, to help them to do their job better. Education really is for life!

Adults Learning How to Fix Cars, Kenya

A Volunteer Teacher, Lesotho

Volunteer Teachers

All around the world, there are volunteer teachers. Doing voluntary work is a wonderful way to see new places and meet new people. Volunteers also help many children and adults to learn information that can help them through their life.

Volunteer teachers work in different ways. Some volunteers move to another country to teach there for a few months or years. Others stay in their own country. Maybe they go to a school for just one or two hours a week, to help young children with subjects like reading and mathematics. Maybe they teach their country's language, for example, French, Spanish, or English, to people who move there from another country.

→ Go to pages 38–39 for activities.

3 Food for Everyone

Some people are lucky because they have many different types of food to eat. In other places, people can't always grow or buy all the food that they need. Many people work to try to provide food for everyone.

Growing Food

Healthy food helps people to stay well because it has lots of important nutrients. When people grow food, they help themselves and other people, too. Some people have a garden or other land where they can grow fruit and vegetables for family and friends. Maybe they can't provide all the food that they all need, but they can help.

Growing Food Together, Tanzania

The World's Main Crops in 2007

metric tons

- 1,800,000,000
- 1,600,000,000
- 1,400,000,000
- 1,200,000,000
- 1,000,000,000
- 800,000,000
- 600,000,000
- 400,000,000
- 200,000,000

sugar cane   corn   rice   wheat

Farmers grow most of the food that people eat. In Asia, farmers grow a lot of rice, and in Europe, they grow a lot of wheat. In North America, farmers grow a lot of corn – almost 50% of all the corn that's grown in the world. The chart above shows that in 2007, more sugar cane was grown in the world than any other crop. About 30% of sugar cane is grown in Brazil.

Farmers also grow vegetables like potatoes, carrots, and onions, and fruits like apples, oranges, and bananas. Some farmers raise animals so that people can eat meat like chicken and beef.

Selling Food

We all need people who sell food. Small, local stores sell food. Markets and supermarkets sell a lot of food. People even sell food on the Internet!

Corn Crops Destroyed by a Storm, Nicaragua

Not Enough Food

People in some parts of the world have as much food as they need to be healthy. People in other parts of the world don't have enough to eat and, sometimes they are so hungry that they can die.

In some places, people can't grow crops because the weather is too hot and dry, or too wet. This often means that they don't have enough to eat. Sometimes, people can't buy food because of a war, or a natural disaster like a bad storm. Maybe food is too expensive and people don't have enough money to feed themselves and their families.

Discover!

Around the world, more than one billion people don't have enough food. Without food and water, people can die after only four weeks.

Helping Hungry People

Many people work to help others who don't have enough food. Some charities give people seeds, so that they can grow food. Experienced farmers teach other farmers how to grow the strongest, healthiest crops, like corn or sugar cane. Some charities help farmers to become Fairtrade farmers. Fairtrade farmers usually sell their crops straight to stores and supermarkets, so that the farmers get more money. This helps them to buy more seeds and to grow more food. Now scientists are even making seeds that can grow with little water.

Discover!

In some countries, scientists have learned to make rain! They put special chemicals into very cold clouds.

→ Go to pages 40–41 for activities.

4 Water for Everyone

Our planet Earth and almost everything on it needs water. Without water, plants, animals, and people would die. In some places, there's a lot of water. In other places, there isn't enough water, and this makes life very difficult.

How Water Is Used

This chart shows how fresh water is used by people around the world. A lot of water is used for farming. Crops need water to grow, and animals drink water. In industry, people use water to help machines to work, and so that they can make the things that we need and enjoy. Water is also important at home. We drink water. We use water to wash ourselves, clothes, and dishes, and to clean the home. We also use water when we flush the toilet.

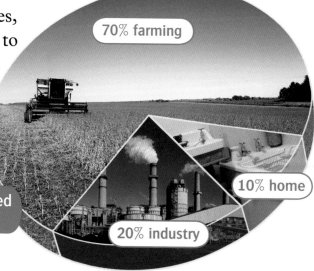

How Fresh Water Is Used Around the World

70% farming

10% home

20% industry

Working with Water

Many people work to provide water for farming and industry, and for the home. Most of the fresh water that people use comes from rivers, lakes, or under the ground. People build reservoirs to store this water. They also build pipes to take it to different places.

In places where there isn't enough water, volunteers sometimes work with local people to build wells to provide water for families. They also help to keep water in wells and springs as clean as possible.

Building a Well, Mali

Most of Earth's water is salt water in the oceans or frozen into ice. Only about 1% can be used by people for drinking, cooking, washing, farming, and industry.

Cleaning Water, France

Clean Water

If people drink or touch dirty water, they can get very sick. People need clean water to stay healthy. People in richer countries are lucky, because they have all the clean water that they need. In the water industry, people use chemicals to clean the dirty water that people have used.

In many poor countries, people have no clean water. Every day, they have to use dirty water for cooking, drinking, and washing. More than one billion people don't have clean water to drink.

Discover!

In some countries, charities give people LifeStraws®. LifeStraws® make dirty water clean and safe to drink.

Collecting Water, India

Saving Water

Today, there are about six billion people on our planet. Every day, there are more! Many people don't have enough water, or they have to travel a long way to collect water.

We need to do things now to make sure that people in the future will have enough water. We can all help to save water. Don't use too much water when you wash your hands and face, brush your teeth, and wash the dishes. Turn off the water when you have enough. Put water in the refrigerator, so that you don't have to turn on the water and use lots of it every time you want a cold drink. Take a shower, not a bath. If you have to take a bath, don't fill the bathtub.

→ Go to pages 42–43 for activities.

Helping in Emergencies

Some emergencies are because of a natural disaster like a tsunami or an earthquake. Others are because of something that people do, like fighting in a war. In emergencies, people need help very quickly.

Help for Refugees

People become refugees when they have to leave their home in an emergency or when their home is lost. There are millions of refugees in the world. Most refugees have had frightening experiences. They have often lost everything – their home, their job, and their school. Maybe they have lost people in their family, too. They often live in refugee camps – special places where refugees can live and be safe.

A Refugee Camp, Pakistan

Charity Workers Giving Refugees Food, Zaire

Refugees try to help themselves, but this can be very difficult. They usually need help from others, too. Refugees need food, water, and somewhere to live. They also need to see a doctor if they have been hurt or if they are sick.

Sometimes a country's government cares for refugees. International organizations like the United Nations usually help, too. Charities are also important. Some charities help to build refugee camps, and to give refugees food and clothes. Other charities help people who are hurt or sick. Charities also help refugees to go back to their home when it's safe.

The Tsunami in Indonesia, 2004

One of the worst natural disasters happened in Indonesia on December 26th in 2004. A huge earthquake under the Indian Ocean caused a giant wave, or tsunami, that traveled thousands of kilometers across the ocean at great speed. By the end of that day, more than 150,000 people had died. Many thousands more people were hurt, and millions of people in many countries lost their homes.

Lots of people helped after the tsunami. Families, friends, and neighbors helped each other. Many people came from countries all around the world to help, too. Governments sent workers to help, and charities sent volunteers.

One of the biggest jobs was to clean up the beaches and towns. People saved things like wood and stones, to build new homes and buildings.

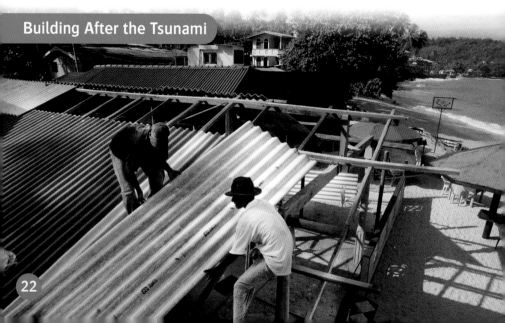

Building After the Tsunami

The Earthquake in Haiti, 2010

Another terrible natural disaster happened on January 12th in 2010. There was a huge earthquake near Port-au-Prince, the capital of Haiti. More than 250,000 homes were damaged, and thousands of other buildings were destroyed. More than 200,000 people died, about 300,000 more people were hurt, and more than a million people lost their homes.

The people of Haiti worked with many people from other countries who came to help. One of the most important jobs was to care for people who had been hurt, and to find people who were lost. Dogs also helped to rescue people from under damaged buildings. People helped to get food and clean water to everyone, and medicines to people who were sick. They also made refugee camps for people who had lost their homes.

→ Go to pages 44–45 for activities.

23

6 Caring for Animals

There are more than six billion people in the world, but there are very many more animals. Lots of people help animals. Do you know any people who help animals?

Vets

Veterinarians, or vets, care for animals. Some vets work in veterinary centers in towns and cities. People take their pets, like cats and hamsters, when they are sick or hurt, or for vaccinations. Other vets go to farms, wildlife parks, and zoos to care for animals.

Discover!

These vets are caring for a snow leopard in a zoo. Snow leopards are very rare – there are only about 4,500 wild snow leopards in Asia.

Animal Charities

There are lots of animal charities. Some charities are small, and they help local animals. Other charities are large, international organizations that help animals all around the world. Charities help animals in many ways, but they need money to do this. Many people give money to animal charities. Some people give money to adopt an animal – the animal stays in its home, but the charity uses the money to help to keep it safe.

Some volunteers from an animal charity in Germany collect toads that are migrating near dangerous roads. Then they take them to a safer place.

Volunteers Helping Toads, Germany

Feeding Orang-Utans, Indonesia

An animal charity in Indonesia helps young orang-utans when their parents have been killed by hunters. Volunteers care for the young orang-utans. They build homes for them, and they feed them. Then when the orang-utans are older, they can return to the forest if it's safe.

Animal Rescue

Some people rescue wild animals. Volunteers rescue animals that are hurt after disasters like oil spills. Birds and fish that are covered in oil will die if people don't clean them.

Caring for a Bird After an Oil Spill, Australia

Whales live in oceans, and they often travel thousands of kilometers every year. Gray whales, for example, spend the summer in the cold Arctic Ocean. Every October, they swim south, and they travel about 120 kilometers every day. Then they spend the winter in the warmer Pacific Ocean.

Some whales swim into water that isn't deep enough. Some swim into rivers or onto beaches. If they can't get back to the deep ocean, they become very tired, and they can hurt themselves. Volunteers try to move them into deeper water. Lots of volunteers are needed and it can take a long time because whales are so big and heavy. If people didn't help whales like these, they would die.

Rescuing a Whale, Australia

Go to pages 46–47 for activities.

Protecting Life on Earth

7

There are many millions of species of plant and animal. They live all around us – on land, in water, and in the air! Without them, Earth and everything on it would die.

Important Species

Species are important in many ways. All species need each other. Animals eat plants, and some animals eat other animals, too. People eat plants and animals. People also use plants as medicines, and in industry.

Scientists Counting Insects, Costa Rica

Protecting Species

All individual plants and animals die, but when every plant or animal in a species has died, the species is extinct. This means that it's lost forever. When one species dies, maybe others that need it will die, too. People need to protect all the plants and animals on Earth. If they don't, many species will become extinct in the future.

Discover!

Scientists think that from 150 to 200 species become extinct every day, but they keep finding new species, too.

Lots of people work to protect Earth's plants and animals. Conservationists work to protect species that are threatened. They work all around the world, in places like rainforests, deserts, and oceans. In the USA, conservationists move sea turtle eggs from busy beaches to quieter places where they can hatch safely.

Protecting Sea Turtle Eggs, USA

29

Protecting African Elephants, Kenya

Elephants live in many African countries. People and elephants have lived near each other for thousands of years. People have killed elephants for meat and for ivory, and they have taken land from elephants, too. They have cut down trees and bushes that elephants need for food, so that they can build houses and grow crops. Sometimes, elephants break buildings, or hurt or kill people, because the people live on elephants' land. This then makes people kill more elephants. Animal charities try to help elephants. They care for young elephants when their parents have been killed by hunters.

Today, more than 16,000 species are threatened, like African elephants and many types of sea turtle. A charity called WWF works to protect threatened species all around the world.

Planting Trees, USA

How Can We Help?

We can all help to protect plants and animals in small ways. When we go out for a walk, we should always leave flowers where they grow. Then, in the future, more plants will grow from the seeds. In gardens and parks, we can grow plants that animals need for food and homes. All these things will help to protect important species.

Discover!

People can build an insect hotel and give insects a safe home! Scientists think that there are about ten quintillion insects on Earth. That's 10,000,000,000,000,000,000 — ten million, million, million!

→ Go to pages 48–49 for activities.

8 Helping Our Planet

For millions of years, there has been life on our planet Earth. Earth has everything that people, animals, and plants need – air, water, and land. Everyone should care for our planet.

How People Damage Earth

People damage Earth with pollution that comes from vehicles like cars and planes, and from electricity used at home and in industry. To make electricity, people burn fossil fuels, like coal and oil. This makes too many gases like carbon dioxide, and they make Earth too warm. Many scientists think that this is changing Earth's climate. Some countries are becoming colder and wetter. Others are becoming hotter and drier.

People use a lot of land to build towns and cities. They cut down millions of trees to clear land, so that they can grow crops and keep animals.

All these things can damage the environment, and many of Earth's species of plants and animals.

Protecting the Environment

Governments, charities, and individuals are working to find ways to protect the environment. Environmental campaigners teach people about problems like pollution. They talk to governments and news reporters. They tell people about ways to stop pollution.

Many volunteers help to protect the environment after a disaster. For example, they clean beaches after an oil spill, or they plant new trees after a fire.

Cleaning After an Oil Spill, South Korea

A Biogas Bus, Belgium

Some scientists have found ways to make clean electricity that does not use fossil fuels. Instead, they use energy from the sun, wind, or water. This is important, because we all need electricity, but there won't be fossil fuels forever.

Today, most cars, buses, and trucks use gasoline that's made from oil. Some engineers have designed cars and buses that use biogas instead. Biogas can be made from waste, or from plants.

Other Ways to Help Earth

If we all use less electricity, we will use fewer fossil fuels. This will reduce pollution. When we aren't watching television or using the computer, we should remember to turn them off. When we go out of a room, we should turn off the lights, too. We shouldn't use very hot water to wash ourselves or our clothes because we use a lot of electricity to heat water.

We all need things like beds, chairs, and tables, but many people buy too much. Making lots of new things uses lots of electricity. We should use things for as long as possible. This will use less electricity. We should also reuse or recycle things as much as possible. This will make less waste, which is good for the environment.

When you turn off electricity, you can help to keep seals safe! Harp seals have their babies on the ocean ice in the Arctic. If Earth gets warmer, the ice will melt and the seals could be threatened.

In small ways, we can help the environment in a big way. We can all help our planet!

A Harp Seal and Her Baby

→ Go to pages 50–51 for activities.

1 Caring for Others

← Read pages 4–7.

1 Circle the correct words.

1 In many countries, the **accident** / **government** helps to care for people.

2 **Midwives** / **Careworkers** bring babies into the world.

3 Care **workers** / **Surgeons** do difficult operations.

4 A **dentist** / **hospice worker** cares for people's teeth.

5 Someone who gives time freely to help others is a **voluntary** / **volunteer**.

2 Find four jobs. Then write four more jobs that you know.

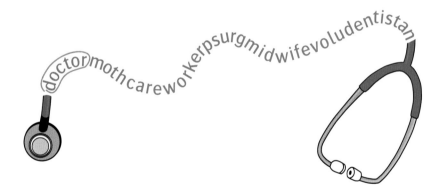

doctormothcareworkerpsurgmidwifevoludentistan

1 ___doctor___   5 _____

2 _____   6 _____

3 _____   7 _____

4 _____   8 _____

3 **Match. Then write the sentences.**

A doctor	cares for someone's teeth.
A hospice worker	helps a baby to be born.
A dentist	helps someone who is sick.
A midwife	cares for someone at home or at a care home.
A care worker	helps people at the end of their life.

1 _A doctor helps someone who is sick._

2 _____

3 _____

4 _____

5 _____

4 **Answer the questions.**

1 When do people get help from doctors?

   People get help from doctors when they are sick.

2 Where do doctors often work?

   _____

3 What do nurses do?

   _____

4 Why do people go to the dentist?

   _____

5 Who can do voluntary work?

   _____

2 Teaching Others

← Read pages 8–11.

1 Write the words.

art   Information Technology   ~~mathematics~~
geography   science   languages   history

1 _mathematics_   2 _____

3 _____   4 _____   5 _____

6 _____   7 _____

2 Write about your favorite subjects. Why do you like them?

1 My favorite subject is _____. I like it because

_____

_____

2 My next favorite subject is _____

_____

_____

3 Complete the sentences.

assistants   teachers   volunteer
Education   university   information

1 _Education_ helps people to do a better job.

2 School _____ get children ready for adult life.

3 Classroom _____ help children who are disabled.

4 After school, many young people go to college

or _____ .

5 Trainers teach workers new _____ to help them to
do their job better.

6 All around the world, there are _____ teachers.

4 Answer the questions.

1 Who teaches children at home?

_____

2 What do teachers help very young children to do?

_____

3 What do playground assistants do?

_____

4 Who teaches college and university students?

_____

5 Would you like to teach others? Why / Why not?

_____

_____

3 Food for Everyone

← Read pages 12–15.

1 Circle the correct words.

1 Healthy **food** / **feed** helps people to stay well.

2 Some people grow food in a **market** / **garden**.

3 **Farmers** / **Teachers** grow most of the food that people eat.

4 In Asia, farmers grow a lot of **rice** / **wheat**.

5 Farmers grow vegetables and **friends** / **fruits**.

6 Sometimes, **stores** / **charities** give people seeds.

2 Complete the chart.

rice potatoes apples oranges onions
sugar cane wheat carrots corn bananas

Crops	Fruits	Vegetables
rice		

3 Complete the sentences.

animals   Brazil   oranges   seeds
supermarkets   Europe   food

1 Some people are lucky because they have many different

   types of _____ to eat.

2 In _____, farmers grow a lot of wheat.

3 In _____, farmers grow a lot of sugar cane.

4 Farmers grow fruits like apples, _____, and bananas.

5 Some farmers raise _____.

6 People can buy food in stores, markets, and _____.

7 Scientists are making _____ that can fight
   plant diseases.

4 Answer the questions.

1 Why does healthy food help people to stay well?

   _____

2 Where can people grow food for family and friends?

   _____

3 What are the main crops that farmers grow?

   _____

4 What types of meat can people eat?

   _____

5 How many people in the world don't have enough food?

   _____

4 Water for Everyone

← Read pages 16–19.

1 Write the words.

home clothes ~~water~~ wells shower water

1 save _____water_____
2 wash _____
3 clean the _____
4 drink _____
5 build _____
6 take a _____

2 Complete the sentences.

shower industry reservoirs water
industry pipes wash safe

1 Without _____, people, animals, and plants would die.

2 Water is important for farming and _____.

3 We use water to _____ ourselves, clothes, and dishes.

4 Water is stored in _____.

5 Water is taken to different places in _____.

6 In the water _____, people use special chemicals to clean water.

7 LifeStraws® make dirty water _____ to drink.

8 To save water, take a _____, not a bath.

3 Answer the questions.

1 Why do people use water in industry?

_____

2 Where does most of the fresh water that we use come from?

_____

3 Why do people build wells?

_____

4 Why is clean water important?

_____

5 How many people are there on our planet today?

_____

6 How many people don't have clean water to drink?

_____

4 How do you use water?

_____

_____

_____

_____

5 How can you save water?

_____

_____

_____

_____

5 Helping in Emergencies

← Read pages 20–23.

1 Write the words.

1 g^{e}c$_e$r$_n_m^{y}_e$ <u>emergency</u>

2 ^{e}h$_u$tq$_e_a$ka^r _____

3 efe^{g}u$_r$e m$_a$^{c}p   _____

4 $_m$e^{v}tg^r^{o}n^e$_n$ _____

5 ^{n}$_o$$_r$itei$^t_n$$_a^{l}_n_a$ _____

6 s^{m}at$_u$i^n _____

2 Complete the sentences.

> help   hurt   emergency   clothes   tsunami
> disaster   camps   refugees   earthquake

1 An _____ is when something dangerous happens.

2 In an emergency, people need _____ very quickly.

3 When people have to leave their home, or when their home is lost, they become _____.

4 Refugees often live in refugee _____.

5 Refugees need to see a doctor if they have been _____.

6 Charities often give refugees food and _____.

7 In 2004, a serious _____ caused a _____.

8 In 2010, another terrible natural _____ happened.

3 Order the words. Then write *true* or *false*.

1 Some / because / emergencies / are / war. / of

<u>Some emergencies are because of war.</u>   <u>true</u>

2 world. / refugees / There / aren't / in / many / the

_____   _____

3 very / life / easy. / A / refugee's / is

_____   _____

4 250,000 / About / damaged / were / homes / Haiti. / in

_____   _____

5 Dogs / to / people. / helped / rescue

_____   _____

4 Answer the questions.

1 Who sent volunteers to help after the tsunami?

_____

2 What did people save to build new buildings after
the tsunami?

_____

3 When did the terrible earthquake in Haiti happen?

_____

4 How many people lost their homes after the earthquake?

_____

5 How did people help after the earthquake?

_____

6 Caring for Animals

← Read pages 24–27.

1 Write the words.

> orang-utan   whale   hamster   bird
> toad   fish   cat   snow leopard

1 _____

2 _____

3 _____

4 _____

5 _____

6 _____

7 _____

8 _____

2 Write about your favorite animal. Why do you like it?

_____

_____

_____

_____

_____

3 **Match. Then write the sentences.**

There are many more	in veterinary centers.
Some people give money	are very rare.
Vets care	animals than people.
Some vets work	animal charities.
Snow leopards	for animals.
There are lots of	to adopt an animal.

1 _____

2 _____

3 _____

4 _____

5 _____

6 _____

4 **Answer the questions.**

1 Why do volunteers collect toads in Germany?

_____

2 How do volunteers help orang-utans in Indonesia?

_____

3 Why do volunteers rescue animals after an oil spill?

_____

4 What do volunteers try to do when whales swim into rivers?

_____

7 Protecting Life on Earth

1 Circle the correct words.

1 There are millions of **species** / **farms** of plant and animal.

2 When a plant or animal becomes **threatened** / **extinct**, it's lost forever.

3 Today, more than **16,000** / **10,000** species are threatened.

4 Conservationists protect species that are **threatened** / **extinct**.

2 Order the words. Then answer the questions.

1 species / What / all / need? / do

   What do all species need?
   All species need each other.

2 people / do / plants / What / for? / use

   _____

   _____

3 does / What / protect? / WWF

   _____

   _____

4 many / are / on / How / insects / there / Earth?

   _____

   _____

3 Complete the sentences.

flowers   home   animals   seeds   protect

1 We can all help to _____ plants and animals in small ways.

2 When we go out for a walk, we should leave _____ where they grow.

3 More plants will grow from a flower's _____ .

4 We can grow plants that _____ need for food and shelter.

5 An insect hotel gives insects a safe _____ .

4 Answer the questions.

1 Why do conservationists move sea turtle eggs?

_____

2 Why have people killed elephants?

_____

3 How do charities help elephants?

_____

5 How can you help to protect plants and animals?

_____

_____

_____

_____

_____

8 Helping Our Planet

← Read pages 32–35.

1 Write the words.

1 l^oc_a _____

2 t^ah_Er _____

3 il^o _____

4 r_{ia} _____

5 n_al^d _____

6 u^{ns} _____

7 d^n_iw _____

8 ta^r_we _____

2 Order the words. Then write *true* or *false*.

1 everything / plants / Earth / and / animals / need. / that / has

_____ _____

2 damage / People / don't / Earth / pollution. / with

_____ _____

3 Too / much / climate. / changing / Earth's / is / carbon dioxide

_____ _____

4 colder / becoming / countries / and wetter. / Some / are

_____ _____

5 build / cities. / don't / need / and / to / People / land / towns / much

_____ _____

3 Complete the sentences.

much   environment   electricity
chairs   recycle   tables

1 In small ways, we can help the _____ in a big way.

2 Many people buy too _____ .

3 We all need things like beds, _____ , and _____ .

4 Making things uses lots of _____ .

5 We should reuse and _____ as much as possible.

4 Answer the questions.

1 Why do people burn fossil fuels?

_____

2 What do most cars, buses, and trucks use today?

_____

3 What can some buses and cars use instead?

_____

4 What should we do to use less electricity when we aren't
   watching television or using the computer?

_____

5 What will happen if we all use less electricity?

_____

6 How can people make less waste?

_____

A Job That Helps Others

1 Choose a job that helps others.

2 Use books or the Internet to look for information.
Then write notes.

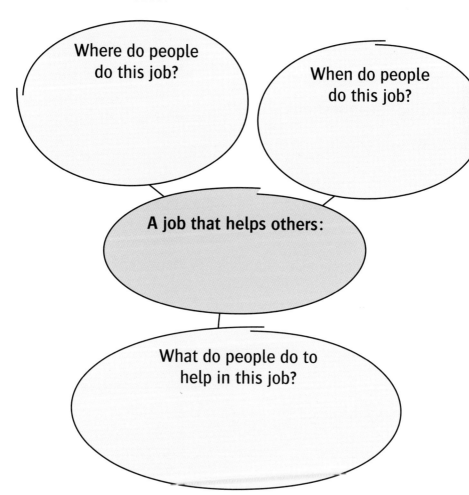

Where do people
do this job?

When do people
do this job?

A job that helps others:

What do people do to
help in this job?

3 Use the information to write sentences about the job.
Display your work.

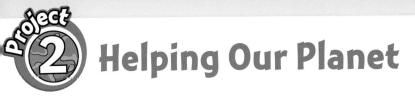

Helping Our Planet

1 Design a poster about helping our planet. Write notes.

What will your poster be about?

Stopping pollution ☐

Protecting animals ☐

Protecting plants ☐

How big will your poster be?

_____

What will the title of your poster be?

_____

What three things will your poster say?

_____

_____

_____

What pictures will your poster have?

_____

_____

2 Make your poster. Write sentences and add pictures.
Display your poster.

Glossary

accident something that happens by chance

adopt to care for a child or an animal when the parents can't do this

adult a person who is 18 years old or older

assistant a person who helps another person in their job

biogas a fuel made from waste, that can be used in cars and buses

capital the main place in a country

care home a place where old, sick, or disabled people live together

care worker a person who cares for someone who is old, sick, or disabled

carrot a long, orange vegetable

cause to make something happen

center a place that's used to do something, for example, care for animals

change to become different; to make something different

charity (*plural* **charities**) a group of people who collect money to help people or animals

chemical a solid or liquid that is made by chemistry

child a very young person

climate the usual type of weather in a place

coal a hard, black fossil fuel

conservationist a person who works to protect the environment

corn (*also* **maize**) a plant that is grown for its grain

cover to put something over something

crop a plant that we grow in large amounts

damage to make something bad or weak

deep going a long way down

destroy to damage something very badly

die to stop living

disabled not able to use part of the body

disaster something very bad that damages Earth, people, or animals

disease a medical problem that makes you sick

earthquake when the ground moves

education teaching and learning, usually in school, college, or university

electricity a type of energy

emergency something serious and dangerous

enough how much we want or need

environment where people, plants, and animals live

environmental campaigner a person who works to protect the environment

extinct when a species has died

Fairtrade the Fairtrade Foundation helps farmers to earn enough money

flush to use water to clean the toilet

fossil fuel things like coal and oil, that come from animals or plants that are millions of years old and found under the land

fresh clean and cool

gas not a solid or a liquid; like air

gasoline (*or* **petrol**) a liquid that burns and powers an engine

government the people who say what happens in a country

grow to plant seeds or plants; to get bigger

hatch to come out of an egg

healthy not sick

hospice a place where people can be cared for when they are going to die soon

huge very big

hurt to give pain; to be in pain

individual one person or thing

industry the production of things, often in factories

information what you know about something

Information Technology studying or using computers

insect a very small animal with six legs

ivory a hard, white material that comes from elephants' teeth

kill to make someone or something die

lake a big area of water

life (*plural* **lives**) the time when you are living

local near to where someone lives

main the largest or most important

market where people buy and sell things like food and different products

medication something that you take when you are sick, to make you better

melt to become liquid because of being hot

midwife (*plural* **midwives**) a person whose job is to help a woman to have a baby

migrate to move from one place to another (for animals)

natural comes from nature; not made by people

nutrient something that we get from food to live and grow

oil a liquid fossil fuel from under the ground

oil spill when oil from big boats goes into the ocean

onion a round vegetable with a strong smell

operation when a doctor cuts or opens a person's body, to fix a problem

organization many people who work together to do something

pipe a long tube that takes water to different places

pollution something that makes air, land, or water dirty

poor not rich

professor (*also* **lecturer**) a teacher at a college or university

protect to keep safe from danger

provide to give

raise to feed and care for animals

rare not very many; not very often

recycle to use again, to make something new

reduce to make less

refugee a person who has to leave their home or country because of war or a natural disaster

rescue to save someone or something from a dangerous place

reservoir a lake where water is stored before people use it

reuse to use again

river water on land that goes to the ocean

shower a place where people stand up to wash themselves

special different and important

species a group of the same type of animal

spring a place where water comes out from under the ground

storm very bad weather

sugar cane a plant; sugar is made from this

threatened in danger

town a place with a lot of buildings; larger than a village and smaller than a city

trainer a person who teaches another person or an animal how to do something

university where adults go to study

vaccination a medicine that protects a person or an animal from disease

vegetable a plant, or part of a plant, that we eat as food

vehicle something that transports things or people

voluntary done by people who are not paid

volunteer a person who does a job and is not paid

war when people or countries fight

waste things that we throw away

wave a line of water that moves across the top of the ocean

way how to do something

well a deep place under the ground, where you can get water

wheat a type of plant that people use to make food like bread

without not having something; not doing something

WWF World Wide Fund for Nature; an organization that helps the environment

zoology a subject that people study to learn about animals

Oxford Read and Discover

Series Editor: Hazel Geatches • CLIL Adviser: John Clegg

Oxford Read and Discover graded readers are at six levels, for students from age 6 and older. They cover many topics within three subject areas, and support English across the curriculum, or Content and Language Integrated Learning (CLIL).

Available for each reader:
- Audio Pack
- Activity Book

Available for selected readers:
- e-Books

Teaching notes & CLIL guidance: www.oup.com/elt/teacher/readanddiscover

Level / Subject Area	The World of Science & Technology	The Natural World	The World of Arts & Social Studies
1 300 headwords	• Eyes • Fruit • Trees • Wheels	• At the Beach • In the Sky • Wild Cats • Young Animals	• Art • Schools
2 450 headwords	• Electricity • Plastic • Sunny and Rainy • Your Body	• Camouflage • Earth • Farms • In the Mountains	• Cities • Jobs
3 600 headwords	• How We Make Products • Sound and Music • Super Structures • Your Five Senses	• Amazing Minibeasts • Animals in the Air • Life in Rainforests • Wonderful Water	• Festivals Around the World • Free Time Around the World
4 750 headwords	• All About Plants • How to Stay Healthy • Machines Then and Now • Why We Recycle	• All About Desert Life • All About Ocean Life • Animals at Night • Incredible Earth	• Animals in Art • Wonders of the Past
5 900 headwords	• Materials to Products • Medicine Then and Now • Transportation Then and Now • Wild Weather	• All About Islands • Animal Life Cycles • Exploring Our World • Great Migrations	• Homes Around the World • Our World in Art
6 1,050 headwords	• Cells and Microbes • Clothes Then and Now • Incredible Energy • Your Amazing Body	• All About Space • Caring for Our Planet • Earth Then and Now • Wonderful Ecosystems	• Food Around the World • Helping Around the World